Men-at-Arms • 453

Armies of the East India Company 1750–1850

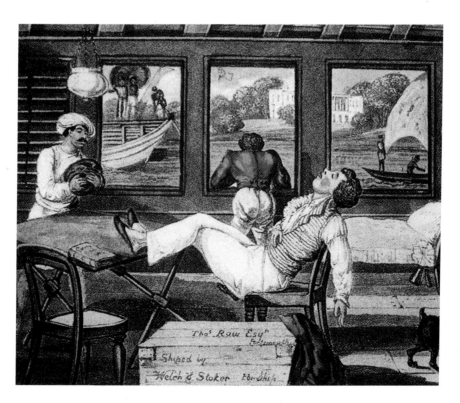

Stuart Reid • Illustrated by Gerry Embleton

Series editor Martin Windrow

First published in Great Britain in 2009 by Osprey Publishing,
Midland House, West Way, Botley, Oxford OX2 0PH, UK
443 Park Avenue South, New York, NY 10016, USA

Email: info@ospreypublishing.com

ISBN: 978 184603 460 2
e-book ISBN: 978 1 84908 096 5

Editor: Martin Windrow
Design: Melissa Orrom Swan, Oxford
Index by Sandra Shotter
Originated by United Graphic Pte Ltd
Printed in China through World Print Ltd.

09 10 9 8 7 6 5 4 3 2 1

A CIP catalogue record for this book
is available from the British Library

FOR A CATALOGUE OF ALL BOOKS PUBLISHED BY
OSPREY MILITARY AND AVIATION PLEASE CONTACT:

FOR A CATALOGUE OF ALL BOOKS PUBLISHED BY OSPREY MILITARY
AND AVIATION PLEASE CONTACT:

Osprey Direct, c/o Random House Distribution Center,
400 Hahn Road, Westminster, MD 21157
E-mail: uscustomerservice@ospreypublishing.com

Osprey Direct, The Book Service Ltd, Distribution Centre,
Colchester Road, Frating Green, Colchester, Essex, CO7 7DW
E-mail: customerservice@ospreypublishing.com

Osprey Publishing is supporting the Woodland Trust, the UK's leading
Woodland conservation charity, by funding the dedication of trees.

www.ospreypublishing.com

Artist's Note

OPPOSITE **Robert Clive (1725–74) was sent out to
Madras as an 18-year-old Company 'writer' or clerk,
but was commissioned an ensign in the EIC forces in
1746 after escaping the French-led capture of Madras
by Dupleix. While he was more of a diplomat than a
soldier, his undoubted boldness and resolution were
the key to his early victories and the EIC's conquest of
Bengal. If Stringer Lawrence was responsible for turning
the Company's European units into proper soldiers, it was
Clive who was the father of the *sepoy* army. As well as
bringing him a peerage, his abilities were recognized by
the rare grant of a regular British Army commission as
well as his EIC commission, and this portrait by Dance
depicts him in the uniform of a British lieutenant-general.
(Unless otherwise credited, all illustrations are from the
author's collection)**

ARMIES OF THE EAST INDIA COMPANY 1750–1850

BACKGROUND

The United Company of Merchants of England Trading to the East Indies, more familiarly known as the Honourable East India Company – or even 'John Company' – was the first and arguably the greatest multi-national corporation the world has ever seen. It was originally engaged in the spice trade of South-East Asia and the East Indies, but by the beginning of the 18th century the main focus of its activities had shifted to the Indian subcontinent, where it maintained three rather precarious toe-holds: at Madras, at Bombay, and at the mouth of the Hugli river in Bengal. Each was governed more or less independently by a council or 'presidency' of the leading merchants, and under the Company's royal charter each jealously maintained its own tiny military establishment, whose sole purpose was to defend the Company's 'factories' – fortified trading posts – from casual brigandage, piracy, or equally weak European rivals.

However, in 1746 commercial rivalry between the East India Company and the French *Compagnie des Indes* turned into outright war, in a reflection of the two home nations' participation in the War of the Austrian Succession on the European mainland and its extension to North America. Both organizations became ever more deeply involved in local politics as they enlisted, bribed and manipulated allies among the Indian rulers. In the end the Company not only emerged from the struggle victorious, but had consolidated and expanded its original modest landholdings to such an extent that it became a territorial and political power in its own right. In the process the unreliable rabble of mercenaries in its service had grown into a formidable army, which by the end of the 18th century was far bigger than that maintained by most European states.

CHRONOLOGY

1600	Original charter granted to East India Company
1698	Charter granted to New East India Company
1702	Agreement to merge as United Company of Merchants Trading to the East Indies
1746	Madras captured by French
Sept–Oct 1751	Capture and successful defence of Arcot, capital of French-allied Nawab of the Carnatic, by Robert Clive of EIC Madras presidency

3

20 June 1756	Calcutta falls to Suraja Dowla, French-allied Nawab of Bengal
2 Jan 1757	Calcutta recaptured by Clive and Adm Charles Watson
23 Mar 1757	French-held Chandernagore captured by Clive
23 June 1757	Battle of Plassey – Clive defeats Suraja's army, securing British-allied rule of Bengal
Dec 1758–Feb 1759	
	Unsuccessful siege of British-held Madras by French Baron Lally
22 Jan 1760	Battle of Wandewash – Lally defeated by Sir Eyre Coote
15 Jan 1761	Lally surrenders Pondicherry to Clive's troops
23 Oct 1764	Battle of Bhaksar – EIC Bengal Army mutineers defeated
1767–1769	First Mysore War – ends in defensive alliance of Mysore ruler Haidar Ali with EIC against Mahrattas
1775–1782	First Mahratta War – ends inconclusively
1780–1784	Second Mysore War – after withdrawal of support of French Adm de Suffren, Haidar Ali's son Tippoo Sahib makes peace
1784	India Act places Company under Government control
1790–1792	Third Mysore War – Tippo Sahib defeated by Gen Cornwallis
1796	Army reformed, with adoption of two-battalion regimental structure and increased establishment of European officers
4 May 1799	Fourth Mysore War – storming of Tippoo's capital Seringapatam by British Crown and EIC troops
1803–1806	Second Mahratta War
23 Sept 1803	Battle of Assaye – British and EIC troops under Gen Sir Arthur Wellesley defeat Doulut Rao Sindhia
1 Nov 1803	Battle of Laswari – victory of mainly EIC army under Gen Gerard Lake
1814–1816	Gurkha War
1817–1819	Third Mahratta or Pindari War – defeats of Jaswant Rao Holkar's armies seal EIC ascendancy
1824	Reversion to single-battalion regimental structure
1824–1826	First Burma War
1825–1826	Siege and capture of Bhurtpore
1834	Coorg campaign
1838–1842	First Afghan War
1839–1840	Capture of Aden
1839–1842	First China War
1843	Conquest of Scinde
1843	Gwalior campaign
1845–1846	First Sikh War
1848–1849	Second Sikh War
1851–1853	Second Burma War
1856	'John Company's last war', with Persia
10 May 1857	Great Mutiny begins with outbreak at Meerut
2 Aug 1858	Government of India assumed by Crown
June 1862	EIC European regiments taken into British Line

THE EARLY YEARS

Madras

At Madras in 1721 the Company had just three military companies, mustering a total of only 545 men of all ranks, of whom only 245 were Europeans and the rest Eurasians. In addition there was also a rather dubious artillery company, ominously known as 'the gunroom crew', which, according to the garrison paymaster in 1724, was 'look on as a lodging workhouse to relieve poor sailors and at the same time be of use to the garrison'. Predictably enough, he also noted that it then comprised 46 Europeans, 52 Eurasians and 30 *lascars* or Indian labourers. What he neglected to mention, as it presumably did not come within his remit, was that this crew were expected to man a total of some 200 guns.

War with France saw a hasty re-assessment of priorities and, thanks in large part to the extensive recruitment of Indian troops, by 1763 the Madras Army mustered some 9,000 men. Over the next 20 years it again increased eight-fold, to 48,000 men in 1782 and – on paper at least – no fewer than 64,000 by 1805. Although Madras had borne the brunt of the war against the French, and later against Mysore and the Mahrattas, this to some extent marked its peak; the wars of the 19th century were chiefly fought by the armies of Bengal and Bombay.

Bengal

By the end of the 18th century Bengal would have grown to be the wealthiest and most important of the presidencies, but in 1756 its military establishment amounted to little more than 150 men, most of whom were Dutch or Eurasian mercenaries. Nearly all were lost in the fall of Calcutta that June, and the subsequent expansion of the army was all the more dramatic in that when Robert Clive arrived at Fulta some months later all that he found was a single volunteer company, largely improvised from the surviving civilians by Captain Alexander Grant. He thus had to create an entirely new army, which he did to such good effect that by 1763 the Bengal establishment amounted to some 6,680 of all ranks. This was only the beginning: in 1782 it numbered 52,400 men, and by 1805 it too had 64,000 men and was still growing.

Modern reconstruction by Bob Marrion of a soldier of the Madras Europeans, c.1755 – see Plate A2. (Courtesy Partisan Press)

Fort William, Calcutta: an 18th century view of the Company's original Bengal fort, unsuccessfully defended in 1756.

Bombay

Until rather late in the day the Company's landholding at Bombay was effectively confined to some coastal islands. It was always an unhealthy and – by comparison with Madras and Bengal – an unprofitable station. With little opportunity for territorial expansion on the mainland, its chief preoccupation was dealing with piracy; rather than building a strong army as the other presidencies were to do, it instead created a navy – the famous Bombay Marine. The land forces required as a simple garrison consequently varied between four and eight rather large companies, apparently mainly recruited from Eurasians. In a return of 1742 they were reported to number 1,593 all ranks, but of these only 346 were Europeans and over 1,000 of the remainder were Topasses – 'hat-wearers', or Indians of Eurasian descent. Significantly, there was no question of racial segregation, and the Europeans were scattered through all eight of the companies rather than being banded together in discrete units.

The army's growth was significantly slower than that of the other presidencies; there were still only 2,550 men on the books in 1763, and 15,000 ten years later. Nevertheless, by 1805, after involvement in the Mysore and Mahratta wars at the turn of the century, there were supposedly 26,500 men of all colours serving on the Bombay establishment.

This dramatic increase in the size of all three establishments was achieved through an equally dramatic shift in recruitment policy. The Company's European units were always fondly regarded as the backbone of its armies, all the way through to their final assimilation into the British Army in the aftermath of the Great Mutiny, but in fact they were always very few in number. Consequently, from the 1750s the Company found itself recruiting and employing ever-increasing numbers of Indian troops – *sepoys* – until in the end its military service could truthfully be described as a Sepoy Army.

CROWN AND COMPANY

This transformation did not come about by chance. It was a direct consequence of, first, the India Act of 1784, which placed the political management of the East India Company under a government-appointed Board of Control; and secondly, of the subsequent appointment of the Marquis of Cornwallis to be Governor General and Commander-in-Chief in India in 1786.

Political issues aside, the Company's problem and ultimately the cause of its failure was that it had never set out to be a military power, and so never fully developed the administrative infrastructure necessary to manage its armies properly. At first sight that might seem to be belied by its apparent success; but it is symptomatic of the problem that it was not until 1807 – a full 50 years after the pivotal battle of Plassey – that a dedicated Military Department was established at its Leadenhall Street headquarters in London. Even then that department comprised just three relatively junior officials; Col James Hanson Salmond, his assistants W.F.L. Stockdale and Capt John Urquhart, and eight 'extra' clerks. To all intents and purposes it was no more than a clearing house for military correspondence, and was very firmly subordinated to the government-controlled Secret Committee.

This lack of commitment was matched on the ground by an inadequate and downright ramshackle officer establishment. At the end of the 18th century the Company's forces were frequently, and not without considerable truth, described as an army of subalterns. In 1784 the 116,110 rank-and-file in the three presidencies were commanded by just 10 colonels and 30 lieutenant colonels, and until the 1796 reforms there was not one single substantive general in the Company's service. This extraordinary state of affairs arose from the simple fact that the Company was reluctant to spend more than was absolutely necessary on its military establishment, so that the sepoy battalions were led by captains, the European battalions by majors and the armies by colonels.

Furthermore, despite the occasional brilliance of Robert Clive and the bravery and determination of other individual officers, the Company's

Major Stringer Lawrence (1697–1775), the father of the East India Company's armies.

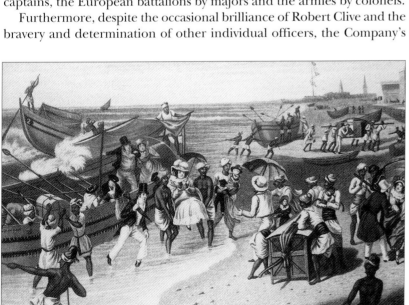

There was no harbour at Madras, and both military and civilian passengers had to be landed from the 'Indiamen' offshore in native boats that carried them onto the open beach. These 19th century travellers are having a fairly undramatic arrival; the surf was often much heavier than this.

Sir Eyre Coote (1726–83) originally came out to Madras as a captain in the 39th Foot, the first King's regiment sent to India; he later commanded the 84th. A Limerick man, he had a knack of upsetting everyone he ever came into contact with, but he was one of the most successful British commanders in the sub-continent.

The India House, Leadenhall Street, in the City of London, shown after it was rebuilt at the end of the 18th century. Although this was the Company's headquarters a Military Department was only created here in 1807.

forces had tended to perform badly when left to their own devices. A hastily-raised expeditionary force from Britain had to bail the Company out after the French seized Madras in 1746. Despite the signing of a Franco-British peace in Europe, continuing hostilities in India required the deployment in 1754 of a regular battalion – Col John Adlercron's 39th Foot – and three companies of the Royal Artillery. As the war against the French escalated yet more units were committed, and although all had been withdrawn or absorbed into the EIC forces by the time hostilities ended in the 1760s, fresh conflicts with the Mahrattas and with the sultanate of Mysore in the 1770s demanded another significant deployment of regular troops to India at that time, notwithstanding the crisis in North America.

The Cornwallis reorganization plan

In the circumstances, by the end of the American War both King George III and his ministers were united in their determination to bring the Company's armies under some kind of proper control. As Henry Dundas at the Board of Control wrote, he 'could not conceive anything more preposterous than that the East India Company should be holding in their hands a large European Army exclusive of the Crown'. However, the plan to reform – or rather, to new-model – the Company forces, as originally devised by Dundas and developed by Lord Cornwallis, was based on a mistaken assumption. It presumed that the most important element was its European regiments and that the sepoy units, although growing in number, were more akin to provincial militia, or – in the classical terms that would have been familiar to Dundas and his contemporaries – were mere auxiliaries to the European legions.

As a first step the Company was obliged to pay for the raising of four new battalions in 1787. These were specifically intended for service in India, but were staffed by half-pay British Crown officers and were ranked as the regular 74th to 77th Foot. Once these new regiments were in place and ready to serve as the core of the new Indian Army, Cornwallis then proposed a complete reorganization of the Company's existing forces. The European forces were initially to be reduced to a single regiment in each of the three presidencies, and subsequently taken into the British Line as regulars. Officers made redundant by the disbandment of the other battalions would then be cascaded out to a newly-created Indian Line comprised of sepoy regiments. They too would hold the King's commission, and would achieve promotion through the same combination of purchase, seniority and brevets for meritorious service as enjoyed by regular officers. Significantly, however, they would not be eligible to transfer between the British and Indian Lines.

Officers' grievances

It fell to Cornwallis' successor as Governor General, Sir John Shore, to implement the reforms in 1796, and he promptly

found himself facing a kind of mutiny. This was not, of course, a bloody uprising, but a rather civilized affair largely conducted by gentlemen through letters, pamphlets and the exercise of personal and collective influence both in India and in London. Neither was it an immediate reaction to the Cornwallis proposals, but the culmination of some long-nurtured grievances.

In the first place, relations between regular officers and Company officers were extremely bad. Before deploying those first regular troops to India in 1754 the British government had prudently obtained a cost indemnity from the Company; rather less prudently, it had at the same time passed a Mutiny Act for India asserting, *inter alia*, that King's officers were to take precedence over Company officers at all times. In so doing it was only following established colonial precedent in North America, where regular officers had always taken precedence over Provincial ones. Cornwallis had reluctantly sought to defuse this particular grievance by awarding local brevet commissions to Company officers, which did not confer permanent rank in the British Army but at least removed the inequality. Unfortunately this still left the Company's officers at a considerable disadvantage: firstly, because their actual responsibilities were very different, and secondly because promotion rates in the regular service were very much faster. This meant that Company officers were still being superseded in their commands by far less experienced regulars.

Bengal sepoys in the 1780s, after a sketch by Solvyns; the man on the left seems to be a *Bhaksari*. Note the so-called 'sundial' turbans – see Plate C1.

The question of comparative rank was not the only cause of resentment. Company officers were always less well paid than their regular counterparts, and could only achieve a satisfactory income commensurate with their actual duties and status through a complicated but prolific system of *ad hoc* allowances. Distastefully denounced by Cornwallis as 'Leadenhall Street economy – small salaries and immense perquisites', the most important ones were summarised by a Bengal officer in 1796:

> The commission upon the Revenues, the emoluments arising from the management of Bazars, and double full Batta when employed upon Foreign Detachments were, with uninterrupted rise from the lowest to the highest gradation of Rank by general Succession, the strong and only inducements which decided our election of the East India Company's service.

The revenue money – a dividend amounting to 2½ per cent of each presidency's net annual revenue – was shared only among the field officers; but the bazaar money, levied on native traders

9

accompanying the army, and above all the Batta or active service allowance, were enjoyed by all. So important was Batta, in fact, that every previous attempt to withdraw it had been met with outright mutiny. There were all manner of other ways, some of dubious legality, by which an officer could supplement his official salary, and all of this combined to make the service an attractive one for those lacking the money or connections to make their way in the regular army. It was bad enough, therefore, that the better-paid regular officers should also demand – and receive – these various allowances; but it was infinitely galling that they should at the same time look down upon the Company men as mere mercenaries and tradesmen, obsessed with making money.

While the officers of the regular army at this time were drawn from a surprisingly wide social spectrum, there is no doubting that in general terms the Company's officers were indeed men who lacked either the connections or the money to enter the King's service. As a contemporary pamphlet written by one of them put it, the Company officers were 'not, generally speaking, men of interest, else we should not have preferred a service in which seniority [i.e. length of service alone] gives command'. Strictly speaking, they did require a modicum of 'interest', since ultimately their initial appointment was in the gift of a Director, who would in his turn have been obliging a shareholder; but thereafter, as the anonymous pamphleteer observed, promotion was strictly governed by seniority within the service as a whole, rather than through a combination of regimental seniority, purchase and merit, as in the regular British Army.

On that principle the Company officers stood firm, and Sir John Shore gave way. The Cornwallis plan was therefore only partly carried through, with consequences that had never been envisaged by either side. The reorganization of the regiments was accomplished, and the European battalions were reduced first to six and then to just three – one in each presidency; but they were not taken over by the Crown, and nor were the sepoy units. Shore did indeed create the Indian Line envisaged by Dundas and Cornwallis, but it remained under Company control. The officers did not become King's officers, and their careers continued to be governed solely by seniority within the service.

John Shipp was a remarkable character who rose from the ranks twice, and although this portrait from his memoirs depicts him in the undress uniform of an officer of the 87th Foot during the Third Mahratta War, 1817, contemporary EIC officers tended to wear the same combination of bell-topped shako, plain dark blue frock coat and light pantaloons. Here going into action, he has discarded the scabbard of his 1796 pattern light cavalry sword, and he carries a pistol in a belt-frog similar to that used by Madras Horse Artillery drivers.

Europeanization of the officer corps

Unfortunately, another aspect of Cornwallis' scheme for reforming the EIC army had far more profound and ultimately disastrous results. Under the old regime the sepoys had been commanded by their own native company officers – *subedars* and *jemadars* – with a European captain and adjutant in overall battalion command. Now the sepoy battalions were to be paired into regiments commanded by colonels, and each battalion was to have a lieutenant-colonel, a major, four captains, eleven lieutenants and five ensigns to command the eight companies. This dramatic increase in the number of European officers might not have mattered had the native

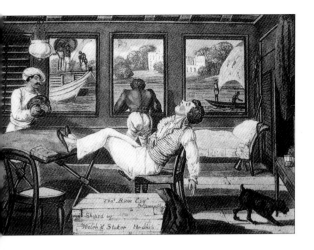

A series of illustrations depicting the adventures and misadventures of 'Tom Raw', a newly-appointed EIC officer cadet, was first published in 1828. Here he is shown on his way to his first posting by *budgerow*, a sort of houseboat that was by far the most comfortable way to travel long distances; and covering a rather less relaxing stage by *palanquin*. The alternative over land was the *dhak gharrie*, a slow and joltingly uncomfortable closed carriage usually drawn by oxen.

officers retained their importance; but the primacy now accorded to European officers, allied to the rigid and slow progression of promotion through seniority alone, meant that the hitherto active native officers in effect degenerated into 'village elders', enjoying a benevolent paternal authority over their military communities but becoming increasingly incapable of exercising effective command.

This sorry state of affairs was compounded by the fact that the increase in the European establishment at regimental level was more illusory than real. Company officials on the ground persisted in the long-standing practice of employing the more able officers on extra-regimental duties – not just on the staff or in command of irregular units, but in the civil administration as well. In 1826, for example, it was calculated that on average only eight or nine officers were actually serving with their battalion at any one time. Moreover, these generally comprised newly arrived subalterns, and those older officers who lacked the aptitude and language skills to qualify for the coveted extra-regimental posts. Since the latter were equally incapable of encouraging their juniors to acquire or cultivate those skills themselves, the inevitable result was the growth of an officer corps almost totally divorced from their soldiers. This process coincided over many years with a growing distance in the relationships between the races, generally ascribed to the more aggressive Christian missionary movement of the new Victorian era, coupled with the arrival in India of many more British women – who demanded a less robust and tolerant social culture than had existed among the Company's expatriates during the 18th and early 19th centuries.

The Great Mutiny

These inadequacies did not, of themselves, bring about the Great Mutiny of 1857, but they certainly made it possible, if for no other reason than that they hampered and ultimately prevented the resolution of grievances among the troops and Indian officers. The causes of the Mutiny were complex, but the notorious issue of the 'defiling' greased cartridges was the final straw. The outbreak was essentially the culmination of a long-running series of resentments exacerbated by an apparently uncaring bureaucracy. Many Bengal sepoys had been recruited in the principality of Oudh, and its annexation in 1856 was a blow to both their pride and their terms of payment. With all of India under the Company's sway there was increasing recruitment of Sikhs and Muslims – considered 'untouchables' by high-caste Hindus – and this coincided with a new regulation that would require sepoys to serve overseas in future. Some units already did so quite happily, but for others it was just one more perceived threat to their religious scruples; this was particularly so in Bengal, where most sepoys were recruited from the higher Brahmin and Ksatriya castes for whom such postings would involve expensive rites of purification. Had regimental officers been closer to their soldiers and more alive to their sensitivities trouble might have been averted or at least contained. Instead, early episodes of insubordination were harshly punished, and a localized mutiny at Berampur in February 1857 was followed by a much larger and bloodier outbreak at Meerut that May.

1820s: 'Tom Raw' discovers that fox-hunting at home has hardly prepared him for the thrills of tiger-shooting. Note the white broad-brimmed hat.

This in turn provided the trigger for much more widespread uprisings, fostered and led by Indian princes resentful of the annexation of their territories by the Company. The war that followed raged savagely across northern and central India for two years, and in the process effectively destroyed the Bengal Army. Of 74 sepoy regiments carried on the Bengal Army List in January 1857, no fewer than 45 mutinied and all but five of the remainder were either disbanded or at least disarmed in order to forestall mutiny. All of the regular Bengal cavalry regiments also mutinied. Perhaps ironically, most of the irregular units, including the Sikhs, proved to be the most loyal of all the Company's forces in Bengal. The Bombay Army, by contrast, escaped almost unscathed, with only two newly raised regiments proving mutinous, and the Madras Army was unaffected.

On 2 August 1858 Queen Victoria signed an Act transferring the government of India to the Crown. Even before the news reached India in November a commission had been set up to determine the future of the Company's forces. A proposal by Lord Canning to massively

Tom Raw is introduced to his commanding officer, a typically elderly gentleman who is rather more assimilated into Indian culture than would be the case in later years.

increase the number of European units permanently assigned to each of the former presidencies was rejected almost out of hand; instead, in June 1860 Cornwallis' long-ago reform proposals finally began to take effect in full. The Company's European regiments (including additional battalions raised during the Mutiny) were to be transferred to the British Army, and the remaining native units would consolidated into a single new Indian Army commanded by officers holding the Queen's commission – and all but seven of them in each regiment would be Indian.

Tom Raw's story ends with a nasty thigh wound during his first battle. By this date all the sepoys are depicted as wearing long pantaloons rather than short *jangheas*.

EUROPEAN INFANTRY

The Company was always (rather grudgingly) permitted to recruit soldiers in Britain, but for the most part those willing to enlist at all found the British Army a more congenial prospect; consequently, the Company had to take what it could get. Perhaps apocryphally, one regimental history later claimed that the Council in Madras plaintively complained on one occasion that while it was inevitable that most recruits were found in Newgate jail, trawling lunatic asylums such as Bedlam was going too far. There are no other references to the alleged recruitment of lunatics, but there is no doubt that the majority of those enlisted at home were men who were leaving their country for their country's good. In 1787 Lord Cornwallis, who could never quite forget he had once been a Guardsman, underlined his plea for more British regulars by complaining that 'I did not think that Britain could have furnished such a set of wretched objects', adding the observation that recent drafts for the Company's army had included 'broken gentlemen', former British Army officers, half-pay naval officers and at least one clergyman besides all the usual criminal riff-raff.

In India this unpromising collection was supplemented by the local recruitment of any white or Eurasian (mixed race) mercenaries who came to hand. In the early days these were Dutch for the most part, but for a time they also included significant numbers of French prisoners-of-war, and especially Swiss and Germans from the French service. Most of them proved to be unreliable, and the best recruits, especially in the early days, were in fact former British regulars discharged when their regiments were ordered home. These men enlisted either because they had contracted local marriages, or simply because once they got used to the climate the majority of the rank-and-file found themselves enjoying a far higher standard of living than they might expect in Britain.

The units which became, respectively, the Madras European Regiment, the Bengal European Regiment and the Bombay European Regiment were not at first conventionally organized infantry battalions. Their organisation, or rather lack of it, more resembled that of the Marines, with all the men effectively serving as a pool from which more or less *ad*

This detail from a 1792 view of Seringapatam (properly, Sringapatnam) shows four small figures at lower left. Two, wearing very short jackets or sleeved waistcoats and light infantry caps, may be British regulars; but the leftmost man, wearing a tall white hat and coat turnbacks in a facing colour, is clearly a soldier of the Madras European Battalion.

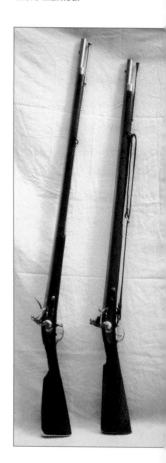

Short Land Pattern (left) and India Pattern firelocks, showing the disparity in size and therefore weight. When the EIC first introduced its own pattern musket in 1764 the difference between its 39in barrel and the 46in barrel of the then current Long Land Pattern was even more marked.

hoc companies and detachments could be formed for specific tasks. Similarly, in the very early days the officers might find themselves commanding European or Indian troops or mixed detachments of both, according to need and availability.

For as long as the East India Company's need was for purely defensive forces, tasked with watching over its 'factories' and escorting merchants and officials, this informal organization was adequate. However, in 1748 the Company appointed a former regular officer, Maj Stringer Lawrence, to reorganize and reform its forces at Madras. This he did by first building up the strength of the existing independent companies, then adding two more recruited in Switzerland, and using an *ad hoc* battalion structure for operations. This became permanent in 1758 with the formation of two more battalions commanded by Capts Polier and Caillaud. Nevertheless, although the Bombay and Bengal Europeans afterwards underwent a similar transformation, and the white battalions would always be regarded as the backbone of the Company's forces – notwithstanding Cornwallis' opinion, unfairly based as it was on their parade-ground appearance – they were always chronically few in number and subject to wild fluctuations in their establishment.

By 1766 there were three European battalions at Madras, and in 1774 they were expanded and reorganized into two regiments each of two battalions, with a third regiment being added in 1777. Similarly, in Bengal the single company commanded by Capt Alexander Grant which served under Clive at Plassey was afterwards expanded into a full battalion, the 1st Bengal European Regiment. In 1778 five more battalions were raised, mirroring the Madras establishment. Bombay was a slightly different case; given its special situation (see above) the organization of its units always tended to be slightly archaic, clinging to the independent company structure for longer than the other presidencies. Nevertheless, by 1788 there were two regiments of Europeans on the Bombay establishment, and this remained the case until 1796 when Cornwallis' reorganization took effect.

EAST INDIA COMP.Y
VOLUNTEER

AN OFFICER SALUTING

The Company even had its own forces in Britain. This Rowlandson illustration depicts a grenadier officer – wearing scarlet, with blue facings and gold lace – of the three-battalion Royal East India Company Volunteers, raised and equipped during the French war from among the EIC's home establishment in London.

In all three presidencies the European regiments were chronically understrength. In 1787 they were some 36 per cent below establishment, and although the Company did its best to ship out enough recruits there was some justification for consolidating them into just one regiment in each presidency. At first each was still allowed to have two battalions, but with a major war then raging in Europe it soon proved impractical to maintain both, and in 1799 all three were reduced to a single battalion apiece.

Not until the subsequent reorganization of 1824, after the end of the Napoleonic Wars had eased the recruiting problem, was it possible to contemplate raising a second European regiment for each presidency, and a third in 1853 – albeit the new 2nd Madras Europeans had to be temporarily stood down for lack of recruits between 1830 and 1840. Although the regiments were still single-battalion formations a degree of flexibility was achieved by deploying them as two separate 'wings' at different stations.

Initially all of these regiments were simply referred to as the Madras, Bengal and Bombay Europeans respectively, but the 2nd Bombay were raised as Light Infantry in 1824, as were the 2nd Madras in 1840, and at the same time the existing 1st Bengal were also designated as Light Infantry. However, in 1843 the three senior regiments were granted quasi-royal status as the Madras, Bengal and Bombay Fusiliers.

On 30 June 1862 all nine regiments formally passed into the British Army, as follows:

102nd Royal Madras Fusiliers (1/Royal Dublin Fusiliers)
105th Madras Light Infantry (2/King's Own Yorkshire Light Infantry)
108th Madras Infantry (2/Royal Inniskilling Fusiliers)
101st Royal Bengal Fusiliers (1/Royal Munster Fusiliers)
104th Bengal Fusiliers (2/Royal Munster Fusiliers)
107th Bengal Infantry (2/Royal Sussex)
103rd Royal Bombay Fusiliers (2/Royal Dublin Fusiliers)
106th Bombay Light Infantry (2/Durham Light Infantry)
109th Bombay Infantry (2/Prince of Wales's Leinster – Royal Canadians)

It will be noted that most of the regiments eventually gained Irish territorial titles under the Childers amalgamations of 1881, not – as is often assumed – as a reflection of their original composition, but simply because most of the Scottish and English recruiting districts were already spoken for.

Soldiers of the Bengal European Regiment, as depicted stacking arms in Capt Abraham James' *Analytical View of the Manual and Platoon Exercises* published in Calcutta in 1811 (see also Plate E2). The shako badges and shoulder distinctions identify the two men on the left as serving in the light company and the third as a private of one of the battalion companies.

Uniforms

The Company's European troops had red coats from the very outset, and while many other details of the uniforms worn in the earliest days are rather lacking, it is possible to build up a fairly comprehensive picture of their appearance in the 1750s (see Plate A2). In general they followed British Army practice, but pictorial evidence indicates a widespread use of tall broad-brimmed hats rather than conventional cocked headgear until the general adoption of military caps or shakos in the 1800s. Stringer Lawrence had previously served in the 14th Foot, and so initially adopted their buff facings for his new command. However, by 1799 the single remaining battalion of Madras Europeans were wearing light blue facings, although Hamilton Smith's chart shows this changed to 'French grey' by 1814, and the granting of the Fusilier title in 1843 was accompanied by a further change to dark blue.

Similarly, a variety of facing colours were displayed in Bengal, but by 1803 the 1st Bengal Europeans were displaying the yellow facings then worn by all infantry units on that establishment. They subsequently adopted sky-blue in about 1822, and then dark blue in 1843, while the 2nd Bengal Europeans raised in 1824 had white. The Bombay Europeans initially had blue facings, but received yellow in May 1792, and subsequently switched to white. The 1st then retained this colour even after becoming Fusiliers, as did the new 2nd Bombay Europeans raised in 1824.

Like those of British regiments the uniforms were further distinguished by worsted lace edgings to collars, shoulder straps and wings, and perhaps to buttonholes as well. In the case of the Madras Europeans this was white with yellow, scarlet and black stripes, while the Bengal Europeans had red and blue stripes in 1809. By the 1840s, however, in conformity with regular practice, all lace was plain white.

NATIVE INFANTRY

Initially the EIC's Indian ('Native') units had their beginnings in irregular bands of locally recruited mercenaries, led by their own officers and carrying their own weapons – *tulwars*, spears, and perhaps matchlocks if they were lucky. They were generally referred to as *peons*, or as *Bhaksaris* in Bengal (theoretically, someone from Bhaksar, but at that time generally used to describe anyone from outside Bengal proper). By the 1750s sheer necessity forced the Company to train and equip its Indian soldiers in European fashion, and to distinguish them from the earlier rabble by using the term *sepoys* instead.

They were still organized in independent companies, but in Bengal the first permanent unit of sepoys was formed by Robert Clive in early 1757 as he scraped an army together around a perilously small contingent of Europeans. They may have fought at Plassey that year as a number of independent companies, but they were soon formed into a proper battalion, later designated the 1st Bengal Native Infantry, and more followed. Profiting by this example, two similar battalions were formed in Madras just before the settlement came under siege in December 1758. During the following year all the Madras companies were grouped into permanent battalions, each comprising nine companies (one of which was designated as grenadiers) with establishments of 115 Indian officers and men. Bombay characteristically lagged behind somewhat, and it was not until 1768 that its sepoy companies were formed into two battalions.

Up until 1796 each battalion was numbered as a separate unit, but in 1796 as part of the general 'new-modelling' of the Company's forces devised by Lord Cornwallis all of them were paired off to form two-battalion regiments, which were then renumbered according to their then seniority; thus, for instance, the 3rd Madras became the 1st Battalion of the new 2nd Madras Native Infantry (MNI). Very largely, however, the measure turned out to be something of a dead letter, since the battalions continued to serve independently of one another. In 1824 there was a reversion to the old single-battalion structure, and consequently another wholesale renumbering.

Sepoy battalions normally included grenadier companies, and in 1783 a composite battalion of grenadiers drawn from the Bombay battalions was taken into the Line as the 8th Grenadiers. This subsequently became the 1st Grenadier Regiment of Bombay Native Infantry under the 1796 reorganization; a second battalion was added in 1798, and over the course of time a number of other sepoy units were also granted grenadier titles in recognition of good service.

Similarly, battalions included light companies, and in some units this was replaced by a Rifle company, dressed not in the regimental uniform but in Rifle-green with black facings. A number of battalions were also

1841: cadets at the East India Company college at Addiscombe, Surrey, in full dress uniforms of dark blue faced with red.

Madras Native Infantry: acquatint after Capt Charles Gold, 1806. (Left to right) a *subedar* or Indian captain and a *havildar* or sergeant, both wearing red jackets faced with yellow, and a *sepoy* in plain white drill order or undress. A similar watercolour depicting *subedars* and *lascars* of the Madras Artillery is said to have been 'sketched at Trichinopoly 1796' but must have been updated, since both show the 1806 pattern turban.

granted Light Infantry status although, as in the British Army, it is often unclear to what extent this was merely an honorific title or whether there was a real difference in training and tactics.

Bengal

In fact very few of the Bengal Army's sepoys were actually Bengalis, but rather Hindus of high caste recruited from the province of Behar and Benares or from Oudh. Starting from Clive's 1st Bengal Native Infantry raised in 1757 (otherwise known as the *Lal Pultan*, Red Battalion), some 21 battalions had been raised by 1764. Three of them – the 2nd, 3rd and 5th – mutinied and were disbanded at Patna in 1763. Rather than leave their numbers vacant as was customary, a renumbering took place in 1764, and again in 1775, when the 18 battalions were organized into three permanent brigades. In 1781 a further renumbering took place, when each was redesignated as a regiment and ordered to raise a second battalion. Thus by 1785 there were 36 battalions, but the reorganization in 1796 saw this number reduced by a third. This reduction was evidently too drastic, for by 1804 three new regiments had been raised, and a further three followed in 1815. Thereafter the size of the Bengal Army increased enormously, until by 1845 there were no fewer than 74 battalions of sepoys.

The rather fluid organization in the early days led to a corresponding series of changes in regimental designations and facing colours, but the basic style of the uniform remained fairly constant. After the 1796 reorganization all of the Bengal Native Infantry had yellow facings, but following the reversion to a single-battalion structure in 1824, and the subsequent expansion of the army, individual facing colours reappeared, as recorded on the accompanying table (see pages 40–41), based on the East India Register and Army List for 1845, just prior to the First Sikh War.

In addition to regulars of the Sepoy Line a number of more or less irregular units were maintained as part of the Bengal Army, the most important of which were the **Local Infantry**. These battalions were chiefly raised in frontier areas and in some ways were a reversion to the old pre-1796 sepoy establishment, in having mainly Indian officers with just a small staff of Europeans to oversee them. One of the most famous was the Sirmoor Battalion, raised from amongst the Gurkha tribes in 1815 (and whose lineage can still be traced today to the 2nd Bn, Royal Gurka Rifles). This unit was entirely typical in having just three European officers in 1845 – the commanding officer, Capt J. Fisher, was seconded from 23rd BNI, the second-in-command, Capt Lumley, from the 2nd Bengal Europeans, and the adjutant, Lt Charles Reid, from 10th BNI. Other units were less successful; for example, the two from Oudh were the surly remnants of the ramshackle army once maintained by the Nawab of Oudh and eventually taken over when the state was annexed by the Company in 1856.

The Local Infantry were dressed in a mixture of styles, often wearing *alkalaks* or the shorter *kurta* rather than coatees, and traditional turbans rather than military ones. In 1845 the following details were recorded:

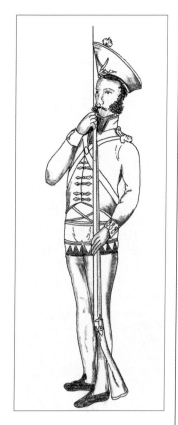

Regiment of Kelat-i-Ghilzie -
Bundelcund Legion — red with blue facings
Calcutta Native Militia — red with black facings
Ramghur Light Infantry — green with black facings
Hill Rangers — red with dark green facings
Nusseree Battalion (Rifles)[1] — dark green with black facings
Sirmoor Battalion — dark green with black facings
Kemaoon Battalion — dark green with black facings
1/Assam Light Infantry — green with black facings
2/Assam Light Infantry — green with black facings
Mhairwarrah Battalion — red with dark green facings
Arracan Battalion — green with black facings
Hurrianah Light Infantry — green with black facings
1/Oude Infantry — red with white facings
2/Oude Infantry — red with white facings
Sylhet Light Infantry — green with black facings
Nimaur Bheel Corps[2] -
Malwa Bheel Corps — green with black facings
Meywar Bheel Corps — green with black facings
Bellochee Battalion -

The drawings in Capt James' *Analytical View...* (1811) are naïve, but full of useful detail. This sepoy of Bengal Native Infantry, shown 'ramming cartridge', has vandyked decoration around the bottom of his shorts, and what appears to be a badge of crossed tulwars on the front of his turban.

The third element of the Bengal Army in 1845 was the **Contingent Forces**, rather similar to the Local Infantry but maintained by client states and commanded by officers seconded from the Company's Line units. Of these the most important was the Gwalior Contingent, a brigade-sized formation comprising seven battalions of infantry, two cavalry regiments and supporting artillery. The other Contingents, from Malwa, Bhopaul, Kotah and Joudepore, were similarly mixed, but each only amounted to the equivalent of a single regiment.

Following the successful conclusion of the First Sikh War a number of units were raised by LtCol Henry Lawrence as the **Frontier Brigade**. Initially this comprised four Sikh regiments recruited at Hoshiarpur, Kangra, Ferozpur and Ludhianah, largely from disbanded elements of the *Khalsa* or Sikh army. In 1847 these were renamed as the 1st to 4th Sikh Local Infantry, and another unit, the Corps of Guides, comprising both cavalry and infantry, was raised at Mardan by Capt Lumsden. In 1851 all four regiments, together with the Guides, were combined to form the **Punjab Irregular Force** and renamed as Punjab Infantry. Once again they were dressed in traditional style, in *alkalaks* and *kurtas*. The 1st Punjab Regiment initially wore dark blue, but by 1856 were in red with yellow facings, as were the 3rd. The 2nd or Hill Regiment had Rifle-green with black facings, and the 4th was in 'drab' – khaki.

---

[1] The Nusseree Bn became 66th Native Infantry (Goorkhas) in 1850, replacing the original 66th BNI, which was disbanded after a mutiny.
[2] Bheels or Bhils are a semi-nomadic people of Dravidian origin. The units were largely employed as police.

Madras

The two battalions formed in 1758 were joined by four more in 1759, and by 1767 there were 19, all bearing the title Coast Sepoys. In 1770 they were renumbered; those in the north were called Circar Battalions and those in the south Carnatic Battalions. This only lasted until 1784, when they were all designated as Madras Native Infantry, with the older Carnatic Battalions having precedence. In 1806 the 1st and 23rd MNI were disbanded following a mutiny at Vellore, their numbers remaining vacant until the general reorganization of 1824. In the meantime, in 1812 the first battalions of the then 3rd, 12th, 16th and 17th MNI were converted to light infantry and given territorial titles: Palamcottah, Wallajahbad, Trinchinoploy and Chicacole respectively. Otherwise the establishment remained fairly stable, and following the reversion to a single-battalion structure in 1824 there were still only 52 regiments of Madras Native Infantry by 1845.

Early references to the dress of sepoy battalions are less than informative, and originally the Madras sepoys at least were dressed in their own predominantly white native-style clothing. In April 1756, however, the Madras presidency advised London of its success in persuading the sepoys to wear 'a uniform of Europe cloth', and a list from September 1759 gives the following details:

First Battalion	red with blue facings
Second Battalion	red with yellow facings
Third Battalion	red with green facings
Fourth Battalion	red with black facings
Fifth Battalion	red with red facings
Sixth Battalion	yellow with red facings
Seventh Battalion	green with red facings

Facing colours changed quite frequently in the early years, but from 1801 they were:

1st MNI	white (disbanded 1806)
2nd MNI	green
3rd MNI	red
4th MNI	orange
5th MNI	black
6th MNI	buff
7th MNI	French grey
8th MNI	bright yellow
9th MNI	gosling-green (dark buff)
10th MNI	red
11th MNI	pale buff
12th MNI	willow-green
13th MNI	feuilemort-yellow (russet)
14th MNI	black
15th MNI	white
16th MNI	pale yellow
17th MNI	deep yellow
18th MNI	Saxon blue (sky-blue)
19th MNI	buff
20th MNI	green (raised 1804)
21st MNI	bright yellow (raised 1804)
22nd MNI	pale yellow (raised 1804)
23rd MNI	white (raised 1804 – disbanded 1806)
24th MNI	pale buff (raised 1807)
25th MNI	bright yellow (raised 1807)

'Sergeant and a Private Grenadier Sepoy of the Bengal Army' by Charles Hamilton Smith, 1815. The private's *jangheas* are noticeably shorter than those worn by Madras sepoys. The sergeant wears *jodhpurs* or pantaloons, originally a privilege of rank granted in 1801 but subsequently extended to all ranks as cool weather dress.

Hamilton Smith appears to show 25th MNI with white facings in 1814 but this is probably a colourist's error. Seemingly unnoticed by him, when the first battalions of the 3rd, 12th, 16th and 17th MNI were converted to light infantry in 1812 they were all ordered in November of that year to adopt dark green facings. As in the other presidencies, the 1824 reorganization was also the signal to change several units' facing colours, and those worn in 1845 are set out in the table on pages 40–41.

Bombay

In 1768 the Bombay companies were formed into two regular sepoy battalions after the pattern established by Clive, and two more were raised over the next two years. In 1777 a Marine Battalion was raised to serve on the Company's armed ships. By 1780 there were 15 battalions plus the Marines. These units were heavily involved in the First Maratha War and the Second Mysore War, but afterwards

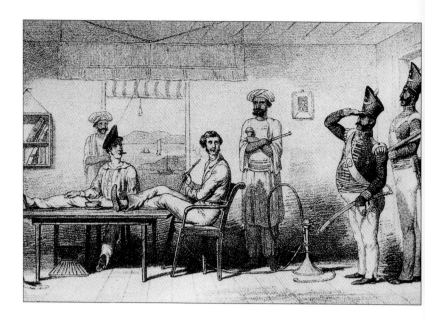

some battalions were disbanded or absorbed, reducing the total to seven, while the 8th were renumbered and named the 1st Grenadier Battalion in recognition of their defence of Mangalore. There was another increase in size in 1788, when five more battalions were raised and all were reorganized into two brigades and renumbered. A further renumbering took place in 1796 when Cornwallis' reforms saw the battalions permanently grouped into regiments. As in the other presidencies there was a reversion to a single-battalion structure which also saw the conversion of the 4th (formerly 2/2nd ByNI) into a Rifle corps. There was also a slight increase in the establishment, but there were still only a total of 26 regiments by 1845.

The Bombay Army affected a certain indifference to the uniform styles favoured by its colleagues on the other side of India. Originally, as depicted in a well-known print of a sepoy of the 3rd Battalion, their turbans were quite unremarkable, but grenadier companies were distinguished by the addition of a mitre-shaped brass plate on the front, rather like those worn by German fusilier regiments. In order to support this the turban assumed a bulbous shape topped with a ball, very similar in some ways to the style favoured by cavalry units (see Plate E3). These were then worn by all Bombay sepoys between 1796 and about 1814, when a more conventional style was adopted, albeit with brass chinscales.

In the early days all Bombay Native Infantry units had yellow facings, but by 1812 they had adopted individual distinctions:

1st ByNI	orange
2nd ByNI	Saxon blue
3rd ByNI	black
4th ByNI	white
5th ByNI	popinjay-green
6th ByNI	light yellow
7th ByNI	pea-green[3]
8th ByNI	pompadour (blue with a purple cast)
9th BNI	pale yellow

'Toast in the Mess'. The toast could be to something quite trivial, since by long-standing convention alcohol was only drunk at table for the purpose of toasts – either general, as here, or by one officer to another.

Following the 1824 re-organisation there was a complete change of facing colours, as listed in the 1845 table on pages 40–41, and the new 4th ByNI, designated as Rifles, had dark green jackets with black facings.

As might be expected, there were rather fewer **local and irregular units** on the Bombay Establishment than in Bengal. These included the Guzerat Provincial Battalion in red coats with light yellow facings; the Candeish Bheel Corps in dark blue coats – probably *alkalaks* or *kurtas*; and the Sawunt Warree Local Corps.

CAVALRY

As always, the cavalry was more expensive to maintain than infantry units and consequently there was at first a certain unwillingness to place it on a permanent footing. During the middle years of 18th century it comprised a number of small and rather short-lived European units, variously listed as hussars and dragoons. The first troop of cavalry was raised in Madras by Lt James Kilpatrick in 1748, but disbanded in 1752. In 1758 a new troop of European cavalry was raised with 2 officers and 36 other ranks. In 1761 three troops of European cavalry were organised, using British troopers in two troops and De Beck's foreign deserters in another, each troop having 5 officers and 60 other ranks. All were disbanded in 1772.

A 1771 inspection report on the 50-odd dragoons stationed at Madras noted that they performed their exercise 'tolerably well' and 'went through the firings and evolutions with spirit and tolerable exactness' (the use of the word 'tolerable' suggesting the very opposite). The inspecting officer was also unimpressed by the fact that while most of their horses were in 'very good order' a few of them were 'rather too fiery, and some appear vicious'. Unfortunately, although he went on to note that their clothing was 'clean and very good', no description was provided.

---

3 Popinjay- and pea-green were very similar, but the latter had a distinct yellowish cast.

The dress of the even shorter-lived units of hussars who appeared first on the Madras establishment and afterwards in Bengal is equally obscure, but was no doubt suitably extravagant. It may have been French in style with a mirliton cap, as many of the men recruited into the original units were German and other foreign deserters from the French service.

Nor were any Indian cavalry units permanently maintained by the Company at this early period, with a rather uncertain reliance being placed on mercenary companies of Indian horse raised, led and equipped by their own officers. These were light cavalry for the most part, but in Bengal from time to time the Company also found it worthwhile to employ 'Mogul Horse' – the subcontinent's heavy cavalry, dressed in a mixture of plate and mail armour and equipped with lance, sword and shield. The first substantive move by the Company to raise its own Native Cavalry came in 1773 with the formation of the Governor General's Bodyguard in Bengal. This was only a single troop, largely employed for ceremonial purposes, but three years later the enlistment of fighting regiments began in earnest.

Madras

In 1767 the Nawab of Arcot placed 2,000 of his horsemen at the disposal of the Company, but following a mutiny over arrears of pay owing from the Nawab's time they were reduced from eight regiments to four. They mutinied again in 1784 when the Company decided to turn them into regulars, reducing them to just one regiment and a handful of men from the others. Notwithstanding this unfotunate start there were again five properly disciplined regiments by 1787.

Unfortunately, early contretemps aside, the numbering of the units initially depended on the seniority not of the unit but its commanding officer, and therefore changed every time one was replaced by act of God or retirement. This state of affairs lasted until 1788, when the newly raised 5th became the 1st and pushed all the other regiments down one place, at which point commonsense was reasserted and the numbers were fixed. One of the regiments was disbanded in 1796 but quickly replaced, and by 1804 there were a total of eight light cavalry regiments on the Madras Establishment.

Uniforms were red from the outset (see Plate B3), and by 1804 all Indian personnel were wearing red dolmans and turbans with white braiding and lace, and the following facing colours:

Sepoy of Madras Native Infantry on parade, 1841; note the bulbous and heavily decorated false turban (see Plate G1).

1st Madras NC	Saxony blue facings (white from March 1811)
2nd Madras NC	dark green
3rd Madras NC	buff
4th Madras NC	deep yellow
5th Madras NC	black
6th Madras NC	French grey
7th Madras NC	bright yellow
8th Madras NC	light yellow

From January 1814, however, the uniform changed completely. The red turbans were retained, but the dolmans were henceforth to be dark

24

(continued on page 33)

THE EARLY YEARS
1: Peon, 1740
2: Madras European, 1748
3: European officer, 1750s

A

CARNATIC TROOPS, c.1785
1: *Subedar*
2: *Havildar*
3: Trooper

1790–1800
1: Bengal sepoy, 1790s
2: Private, 2nd Madras Europeans, 1780s
3: Eurasian fifer, c.1800

C

BRITISH OFFICERS, 1790s–1800

1: Lieutenant-colonel, 7th Madras Native Cavalry, 1790s
2: Officer in hussar jacket, 1799
3: Officer in service dress, c.1800

D

INFANTRY, 1805–14
1: *Havildar*, Bengal Native Infantry, 1814
2: Private, Bengal Europeans, 1811
3: *Sepoy*, 1st Bombay Native Infantry, 1805

NATIVE CAVALRY
1: Farrier, Skinner's Horse
2: *Sowar*, Bengal Native Cavalry, 1814
3: *Sowar*, Java Light Cavalry or 4th MNC, 1812–15

1

2

3

F

THE SEPOY ARMY, 1820–35
1: *Sepoy*, 40th Madras Native Infantry, 1835
2: *Sepoy*, 1st Madras Pioneers, 1835
3: Trooper, 1st Rohilla Cavalry, 1820s

G

H

1846: Rifle and Light Infantry officers in full dress, by Ackerman. One of the European units on each establishment was formally designated as Light Infantry, as were a number of sepoy units. Although the Bengal Army's three Gurkha battalions were dressed as Rifles from the outset they were not titled as such until after the Mutiny. The officer on the left therefore probably belongs to one of the Rifle companies formed within some regiments.

blue, and then from 1817 'cavalry-grey' – although some were still in dark blue as late as 1820. The facing colours were also changed: the 1st and 5th MNC now had pale yellow; the 2nd and 6th, orange; the 3rd and 7th, buff; and the 4th and 8th deep yellow. None were subsequently redesignated as lancers.

No irregular cavalry units were raised in Madras, but in 1826 five regiments forming the Hyderabad Contingent Cavalry were taken under Company control, under the command of British officers. All five had green *alkalaks* lined with white. The British officers assigned to them wore green hussar jackets and light cavalry helmets.

Bengal

Initially the Bengal Army relied on three troops of Mogul Horse, but these were disbanded in 1772 and not replaced until 1776. The first two were disbanded again in 1783, but the third continued as a single troop. A troop of Pathans was formed in 1778, and in 1783 both troops were expanded into full regiments. Third and fourth regiments were raised in the mid 1790s, four more in the early years of the 19th century, and two more in 1825. The 11th was the last to be raised, as late as 1842, as a replacement for the disbanded 2nd. All were officially designated as Light Cavalry, although the 4th were lancers. In addition there was the Governor

General's Bodyguard, which was now formed of picked officers and men drawn from the Light Cavalry regiments rather than by direct recruitment; and a volunteer unit was briefly formed for service on Java (see Plate F3). Otherwise the regular establishment remained stable until dissolved in the Mutiny of 1857.

Additionally, however, no fewer than 18 regiments of irregular horse were raised between 1803 and 1846, largely under what was called the *sillidar* system, which required recruits to provide and maintain their own horses and equipment. A further six regiments were raised in the Punjab: the Guides in 1846, and the 1st to 5th Punjab cavalry in 1849.

At first all of the Light Cavalry wore dark blue turbans, and red dolmans with white cording and braid, with facings as follows:

1st Bengal LC	blue facings
2nd	yellow
3rd	white
4th	green
5th	buff
6th	orange (changed to French grey 1808)
7th	yellow
8th	yellow

In December 1809 all regiments (with the exception of the Governor General's Bodyguard) were ordered to change to French or 'cavalry-grey' dolmans, with red facings for all. In the event a shortage of suitable cloth meant that the changeover was not completed until 1811, and in the meantime the facing colour was officially changed to orange in March 1810. Only the 5th Light Cavalry were excepted, having black facings. The clothing of the irregular horse was much more traditional in style: sowars (troopers) normally wore an *alkalak*, *pyjama* trousers and a *pugri* or turban, and carried a variety of weapons including lances:

	Title	*alkalak*	*pugri*	*pyjamas*
1st	Skinner's Horse	yellow	blue	red
2nd	Gardner's Horse	green	red	
3rd	1st Rohilla Cavalry	red	blue	yellow
4th	Skinner's Horse	yellow	blue	red
5th	Gough's Horse	red	white	
6th	Oudh Auxiliary Cavalry	red	yellow	
7th	Oudh Auxiliary Cavalry	red	blue	
8th	Oudh Auxiliary Cavalry	red	red	white
9th	Christie's Horse	red	yellow	yellow
10th	Bundelkund Legion	blue	white	red
11th	-	scarlet		
12th	-	blue	crimson	yellow
13th	-	blue		
14th	-	-		
15th	-	red	dark	blue
16th	-	red		
17th	-	scarlet		
18th	-	blue	red	red

Officer of the 37th Madras Native Infantry in undress uniform, wearing a red shell jacket with yellow facings; from *Costumes of the Madras Army* (1841).

Guides	khaki	khaki
1st Punjab Cavalry	dark blue	scarlet
2nd Punjab Cavalry	scarlet	dark blue
3rd Punjab Cavalry	dark blue	dark blue
4th Punjab Cavalry	dark green	scarlet
5th Punjab Cavalry	dark green	scarlet

Bombay

In 1803, Colonel John Murray received permission to raise a troop of cavalry; two years later a second troop was approved, but not actually raised until 1816. A year later they were both brought up to regimental strength with drafts from the Madras Cavalry. A third regiment was raised from the Poona Auxiliary Horse in 1820, and in 1842 the 1st Regiment were converted to lancers (see Plate H1). The original troop was dressed in red, but after 1817 cavalry-grey was adopted, and in due course all three Bombay Light Cavalry regiments had white facings.

Four irregular cavalry units were subsequently raised in Bombay, commanded by officers seconded both from the Light Cavalry and from infantry units: the Guzerat Irregular Horse in 1839; two regiments of Scinde Irregular Horse raised in 1839 and 1846; the Poona Irregular Horse in 1847, and the South Mahratta Horse in 1850. All four wore green or dark green *alkalaks*.

* * *

As with infantry battalion colours, each cavalry regiment was allowed three standards, one for each squadron. The first squadron standard had the Royal arms in the centre and a small Union in the upper corner next to the staff. The second squadron standard bore the East India Company's arms embroidered in the centre, while the third was

The enlargement of the two officers in the engraving above (seen at centre left) shows the braided hussar-style jacket (see **Plate D2**) that seems to have been a popular alternative to the 'regimentals' worn by the two officers at far left in the main picture. It was worn not only in the EIC service but also by some King's officers.

Presentation of colours to one of the three Royal East India Company Volunteer battalions in Britain; unlike the Indian units this has the conventional pair, King's and Regimental colours.

Colours

The 1759 List for the Madras Native Infantry provides some information on the early colours but is not entirely clear. It would appear that each company within the battalion carried its own colour, with a Union in the canton, and for the first four battalions a red cross overall to distinguish the grenadier company. The Fifth Bn, having red colours, displayed a white cross overall; and the Sixth and Seventh Bns had parallel stripes rather than their facing colour alone. One early history suggests that the colours were also inscribed with a symbol identifying the Indian *subedar* or captain commanding each company.

This elaborate system did not last long, and in 1777 it was ordered that the only distinction to appear on sepoy colours was to be the number of the battalion and, in the case of the Madras units, an indication as to whether they were Carnatic or Circar battalions (the former being the original units and the others raised more recently after the absorption of the Northern Circars), although this distinction did not last long.

In Bengal the regulations of 1781 stated that 'the first colour of each battalion shall be the great union throughout and the second, the colour of the facing of the regiment; except those regiments which were faced with black, which shall have a white field with the union in the upper canton. The number of the regiment shall be embroidered in gold Roman letters within the wreath in the centre of the middle colour of each battalion.' This confirms that before the end of the 18th century a three-colour system was in place; the first colour was the great Union, denoting that ultimately the regiment was in the service of the British Crown; the second was white, and bore the arms of the East India Company, and the third displayed the regimental facing-colour and distinctions. Both the latter also had a Union in the canton.

of the colour of the regimental facings with a central Union wreath bearing the number of the regiment. In the Madras Army the first or King's standard was crimson, and both the second and third standards were of the colour of the facings. The King's colour was blue in both the Bengal and Bombay Armies, the other two being in the facing-colour.

ARTILLERY & ENGINEERS

Artillery companies were formed in each presidency, initially to man the guns on the walls of the trading-station 'factories', but inevitably they soon found themselves in the field as well. Indeed, by the 19th century the Company's gunners had established a splendid reputation and earned the ungrudging respect of the Woolwich-trained officers of the Royal Artillery.

The early companies were unusual in that the personnel were of mixed race. The actual gunners were normally Europeans, and supposedly the pick of the Company's recruits, but the equivalent of the unskilled matrosses who provided the muscle for moving guns in the Royal Artillery were native soldiers, sometimes referred to in the very early days as *lascars*,

Sowars of Native Cavalry, by Hamilton Smith, 1815. The two mounted figures belong to Bengal Army units: at left, the Governor General's Bodyguard, in red jacket with dark blue facings, and centre, 6th BNC in 'French' or 'cavalry' grey with orange facings – both have dark blue turbans and white lace. The dismounted trooper supposedly belongs to the Java Light Cavalry, but the uniform actually appears to be that of the 4th Madras Native Cavalry (see commentary to Plate F3).

Madras Foot Artillery with a 9pdr gun, as depicted in an 1820s manual. Apart from their cap badges and buttons they are indistinguishable from their British Army counterparts.

Ordnance officer, 1841, wearing a blue shell jacket faced with scarlet; his collar is embroidered with gold oakleaves and his forage cap is trimmed with impressive quantities of gold lace.

but more commonly as *golundaz* – a Hindi word meaning 'carriers of cannon-balls'. Under the 1796 reorganization the gunners and matrosses were separated into separate units for administrative purposes, although continuing to work together in practice.

By 1845 the Bengal Establishment had three brigades of Horse Artillery, each with three European troops and one Native troop. There were also five battalions of European Foot Artillery each with five companies, and two battalions of Native Foot Artillery with ten companies apiece. Madras had one brigade of Horse Artillery comprising four European and two Native troops, and three battalions of European Foot Artillery each with four companies, supported by a single battalion of Native Foot Artillery mustering six companies. In Bombay by 1845 there was one brigade of Horse Artillery comprising four European troops; two battalions of European Foot Artillery, each of four companies; and a single battalion of Native Foot Artillery with ten companies.

From the outset, uniforms in all three presidencies were patterned after those of the Royal Artillery: dark blue coats or jackets with red facings, and yellow lace and cording where appropriate, with the obvious difference that in the early days broad-brimmed hats or topees were worn by European personnel and turbans by Indian soldiers. However, the Horse Artillery uniforms (see Plates G3 and H3) were suitably dashing, and quite outshone their regular counterparts.

Followers

The supporting services of the East India Company's armies were exclusively Indian. In place of a conventional commissariat it was provisioned by a system of bazaars or civilian markets, themselves dependent on itinerant grain merchants known as *brinjarries*. Allowing the individual sepoys to purchase and prepare their own food rather than issue rations avoided the otherwise intractable problems of catering for the special diets required by the various castes and religions, but obviously imposed a heavy burden on operations. In 1781, for example, Sir Eyre Coote started off with some 6,000 sepoys and 15,000 followers, but when he subsequently doubled his bayonet strength to 12,000 men he found himself encumbered by an estimated 40,000 followers. When Gerard Lake took Delhi in 1803 it was reckoned that he had something like five followers for each soldier.

The indispensible *bhistie* or water-carrier – depicted here by Capt Oliver Jones, RN, in 1857 – would later be immortalized in Kipling's poem '*Gunga Din*'.

Not all of these civilians were confined to the bazaars. Cavalrymen (and anyone else with a horse) required a *syce*, a grass-cutter or -puller. The *bhisties* or water-carriers were described by Capt Jones as 'one of the most useful, indeed absolutely necessary servants in India… When one's establishment has got two or three horses in it he has plenty to do, for he has to draw water not only for his master and the servants, and all the cooking, &c., but also for the horses, for they, or their syces, are much too fine to go to a tank to drink.' More importantly, *bhisties* also provided water for the troops on the march and sometimes in action as well.

Engineers

All three presidencies also maintained a separate corps of engineers, made up – as in the British Army – entirely of officers. The actual labouring was carried out by separate Indian companies of Sappers and Miners, which did not appear in the Army Lists but were commanded by Engineer officers.

Officers' uniforms broadly followed those of the Royal Engineers, although there were some original touches. The Bengal Engineers had garter-blue velvet facings like their regular counterparts, while those worn by Bombay Engineers were merely recorded as 'blue', but the Madras Engineers rejoiced in purple velvet facings. In Bengal the original companies of lascars wore dark green with black facings, but the Corps of Sappers and Miners which replaced them in 1819 had red jackets faced with blue, and dark blue turbans. In Madras such companies initially had dark blue with black facings before changing to dark green, and in Bombay they also wore dark green with black facings. Like those in Bengal, they were absorbed into the red-coated Sappers and Miners in 1831 and 1830 respectively, but in Madras at least an 1835 watercolour shows the green uniform still being worn at that date.

Bengal		Madras		Bombay	
Regt	*Facings*	*Regt*	*Facings*	*Regt*	*Facings*
1st BNI	white	1st MNI**	white	1st ByNI Grenadiers	white
2nd BNI Grenadiers	yellow	2nd MNI	deep green	2nd ByNI Grenadiers	white
3rd BNI	bright yellow	3rd MNI Palamcottah Light Infantry	dark green	3rd ByNI	sky-blue
4th BNI	yellow	4th MNI	Orange	4th ByNI Rifles	dark green jackets, black velvet facings
5th BNI	white	5th MNI**	black velvet	5th ByNI Light Infantry	black
6th BNI	Dark green	6th MNI	Buff	6th ByNI	black
7th BNI	Dark green	7th MNI	French grey	7th ByNI	white
8th BNI	yellow	8th MNI	bright yellow	8th ByNI	white
9th BNI	white	9th MNI	dark green	9th ByNI	black
10th BNI	Dark green	10th MNI	Red	10th ByNI	black
11th BNI	white	11th MNI	gosling-green	11th ByNI	buff
12th BNI	white	12th MNI	bright yellow	12th ByNI	buff
13th BNI	Dark green	13th MNI	white	13th ByNI	buff
14th BNI	Buff	14th MNI	buff	14th ByNI	light buff
15th BNI	French grey	15th MNI	orange	15th ByNI	light buff
16th BNI Grenadiers	buff	16th MNI**	black	16th ByNI	light buff
17th BNI	French grey	17th MNI	white	17th ByNI	pale yellow
18th BNI	lemon-yellow	18th MNI	red	18th ByNI	pale yellow
19th BNI	dark green	19th MNI	French grey	19th ByNI	deep yellow
20th BNI	white	20th MNI	deep green	20th ByNI	deep yellow
21st BNI	yellow	21st MNI	pale buff	21st ByNI	deep yellow
22nd BNI	white	22nd MNI	pale buff	22nd ByNI	dark green
23rd BNI	dark green	23rd MNI Wallajahbad Light Infantry	dark green	23rd ByNI	dark green
24th BNI	white	24th MNI**	willow-green	24th ByNI	dark green
25th BNI*	blue	25 th MNI	feuilemort- yellow (tan)	25th ByNI	pale yellow
26th BNI	red	26th MNI**	feuilemort- yellow (tan)	26th ByNI	light buff
27th BNI	red	27th MNI	black		
28th BNI	dark green	28th MNI	black		
29th BNI	dark green	29th MNI	white		
30th BNI	buff	30th MNI	white		
31st BNI	buff	31st MNI Trichinopoly Light Infantry	dark green		
32nd BNI	black	32nd MNI	pale yellow		
33rd BNI	black	33rd MNI	deep yellow		
34th BNI	disbanded	43rd MNI Chicacole Light Infantry	dark green		
35th BNI	white	35th MNI	pale buff		
36th BNI*	lemon-yellow	36th MNI**	pale buff		
37th BNI*	lemon-yellow	37/MN Grenadiers	buff		
38th BNI*	dark green	38th MNI**	buff		
39th BNI*	dark green	39th MNI	dark green		
40th BNI*	blue	40th MNI	dark green		
41st BNI	pale yellow	41st MNI	bright yellow		
42nd BNI Light Infantry	yellow	42nd MNI	bright yellow		

Bengal		Madras	
Regt	Facings	Regt	Facings
43rd BNI Light Infantry	pea-green	43rd MNI	pale yellow
44th BNI	pea-green	44th MNI	pale yellow
45th BNI	dark green	45th MNI	white
46th BNI	dark green	46th MNI	white
47th BNI*	yellow	47th MNI	pale buff
48th BNI	yellow	48th MNI	pale buff
49th BNI	buff	49th MNI**	bright yellow
50th BNI	buff	50th MNI	bright yellow
51st BNI	dark green	51st MNI	white
52nd BNI	dark green	52nd MNI	pale buff
53rd BNI	yellow		
54th BNI	yellow		
55th BNI	white		
56th BNI	white		
57th BNI	light buff		
58th BNI	light buff		
59th BNI	Saxon green		
60th BNI	Saxon green		
61st BNI	yellow		
62nd BNI	yellow		
63rd BNI	yellow		
64th BNI	yellow		
65th BNI*	yellow		
66th BNI*	white		
67th BNI*	yellow		
68th BNI*	yellow		
69th BNI	white		
70th BNI	yellow		
71st BNI	black		
72nd BNI	yellow		
3rd BNI	yellow		
74th BNI	yellow		

THE SEPOY LINE, 1845

Details as taken from East India Register and Army List 1845; Bengal Native Infantry units marked with an asterisk (*) were 'Volunteers' raised for general service and capable of being sent overseas. Madras Native Infantry units marked with a double asterisk (**) included a Rifle company dressed in dark green rather than red.

PLATE COMMENTARIES

A: THE EARLY YEARS
A1: Peon, 1740
A2: Madras European, 1748
A3: European officer, 1750s

The original native soldiers employed by the Company were normally referred to not as *sepoys* but as *peons*, or countrymen, which accurately reflected their irregular and untrained status. Rather than being directly enlisted into the Company's service they belonged to mercenary companies serving under their own leaders, and were indistinguishable in character and appearance from those in the service of native rulers and local *zemindars* or petty landowners. **A1** is based on contemporary watercolours of typical footloose young men of the time; in this case he is properly armed with a musket (albeit a matchlock), although in the very early days *tulwar* swords, shields and spears or lances were rather more common. While adequate for dealing with *dacoits* or bandits, or for casual intimidation, such companies were quite ineffective against properly trained troops. When ordered to take part in a sortie during the unsuccessful defence of Madras in 1746 the garrison's *peons* made a noisy demonstration and then gratefully took the opportunity to get away.

The European companies, as illustrated by **A2**, wore surprisingly practical uniforms in the early days. Soldiers serving in Madras in the 1740s were ordered to be 'new cloathed once in two years with English cloth out of the Company's warehouses'. In June 1748 Stringer Lawrence's orders laid down that while each captain was to be responsible for clothing his company, 'for regularity, the Major [Lawrence] or Officer Commanding the Companys shall appoint a pattern coat and hat or cap suitable to the climate to be approved of by the Governor, and to which every Captain will conform at the first making of the new cloathes… and that the stoppages from the non-commission officers and private men to be no more than is reasonable and that it be made gradually, and in such equal parts as to re-imburse the Captains from new cloathing to new cloathing for his first cost and a moderate profit thereon.' As the red woollen coat was to be 'suitable to the climate' it was presumably unlined, or lined with a cotton material rather than with wool as at home, and was probably cropped short as well. Unfortunately there is no indication as to the form of the hat or cap, but once again the qualification that it was to be 'suitable to the climate' indicates that it was not the familiar three-cornered hat then worn in Europe. It was either broad-brimmed or, rather more likely, the *solar topee* style shown here, taken from a slightly later illustration of a Company artilleryman; this was not made of felt but of white cotton or linen stretched over a rattan framework.

The provision of 'English cloth' probably only extended to the actual coats, as a list of 'necessaries' being issued to troops serving at Trichinopoly in 1755 included Pariar shoes, coarse shirts, coarse stockings, with gingham breeches and waistcoats – gingham being a cotton material which at this time was often striped rather than checked, and usually in blue and white, although it is unclear why this material should be preferred to plain or uncoloured cotton.

Accoutrements appear at this early date to have been of tanned rather than buff leather – probably black – as being better suited to the climate. There is no reference to them in the documents referred to, but the lightweight combination shown here was a popular one amongst colonial troops at this time. A narrow waist belt supports a rather basic bellybox, featuring a simple leather flap fixed directly to a wooden block drilled for seven or eight cartridges, and an equally simple bayonet frog. Knapsacks were invariably carried with the heavy baggage on bullock carts, and canteens were unnecessary as water was supplied on the march and in action by *bhistie* boys carrying goatskin bladders.

Faced with the perennial difficulty of finding enough suitable recruits for its European companies, in the face of what often amounted to official obstruction at home, the Company decided in 1751 to hire some Swiss mercenaries. In July of that year articles were signed with a military entrepreneur named Schaub for the provision of two companies, each comprising four officers, six sergeants, six corporals, a drum-major, two drummers and 120 rank-and-file. All of the men were to be Protestants, and although the contract stated that they were to be raised primarily in Zurich, Geneva and Basle, recruits from Alsace and Hanover were also to be accepted (which in practice meant that Schaub was going to take whatever he could find). Between 1751 and 1754 it seems that about 500 men were sent out, and initially the Company agreed to maintain the traditional Swiss mercenary privileges with regard to discipline, drumcalls and so on. However, the arrangement seems to have lapsed by 1754, and when the various European companies were regimented by Stringer Lawrence the remaining Swiss personnel were fully integrated into the two battalions of Madras Europeans (and in some cases into the artillery) rather than being maintained as a separate battalion.

In action the Swiss generally upheld their high military reputation, but as mercenaries they were nevertheless prone to taking their individual services elsewhere and informally transferring either to the Swiss and German companies in the French service, or to freelancing with the Indian princes. The most notorious was an Alsatian named Walter Reinhardt, otherwise known as Somroo, who gained a startling reputation for ruthlessness during the 1750s and afterwards.

However, **A3** is largely reconstructed from both a portrait and an actual coat belonging to the far more respectable Daniel Frischmann, who went out to India as a cadet with the first contingent in 1751 and survived to return to Basle as a colonel in 1770. Once again it was laid down in 1748 that 'the Major shall appoint the uniforms for the commission officers, to be approved by the Governor'. The coat and waistcoat shown here present something of a puzzle since with the exception of an epaulette on the left shoulder – omitted from this reconstruction – its style strongly suggest a date in the 1750s. Its survival, and the fact that Frischmann chose to be painted in it on his return home, suggest that it was in continuous use throughout his service, but its good condition also suggests that it was reserved only for the most formal of occasions and that something rather lighter and better suited to the climate was preferred for everyday wear. The portrait shows nothing of Frischmann's breeches, but the red velvet ones depicted here appear in an inventory of the effects of a Scottish officer, Capt Robert Bannatyne, killed at Conjeveram in 1759, and are appropriate to the heavily braided formal coat and waistcoat. Interestingly, Bannatyne also had two 'old' regimental coats besides his embroidered one, and five pairs of 'old gingham breeches' as well as a fair variety of civilian garments.

B: CARNATIC TROOPS, c.1785

B1: *Subedar*
B2: *Havildar*
B3: Trooper

This plate is based on a series of sketches of Carnatic (Madras) troops by an otherwise unidentified artist named Green, which all appear from internal evidence to date from some time in the early 1780s. European jackets are now being worn but otherwise nearly all the clothing is still very much of Indian style. They are nevertheless properly equipped and accoutred, and there is no doubt that they are now disciplined soldiers.

Titled by Green as a 'Soubador of Carnatic Sepoys', **B1** is a native captain. By this period British regular uniforms displayed the facing colour, in this case yellow, on the collar, cuffs and lapels only, with the turnbacks of the skirts white. Company troops, however, continued to display their facing colour not only on the turnbacks but also on the shoulder straps and wings. Apart from the silver lace and the fact that he carries a traditional Indian *tulwar* sabre, this man is instantly identified as an officer both by the crimson silk net sash, and also by the wearing of *jodhpurs* or close-fitting trousers rather than *jangheas* or shorts. Note (at his right hip) that under the sash he is wearing a second, more functional, sash or *cummerbund* supporting his jodhpurs; this one is white and the two blue lines visible on the loose end may correspond with the decoration on the bottom of the shorts worn by his rank-and-file.

B2 wears a broadly similar uniform, chiefly differing in the wear of *jangheas* rather than *jodhpurs*; the blue decoration around the bottom of the legs apparently varied from regiment to regiment,although details of the different patterns are unrecorded. He is identified as a *havildar* or sergeant by the silver lace on his uniform and by the silver tassel on his turban, but instead of carrying a sergeant's halberd or other pole-arm he wears the normal infantry equipment of white 'buff leather' cross-belts supporting a bayonet and cartridge box, both of them pushed well round to the rear in approved style. Ordinary sepoys wore exactly the same uniform but with plain white lace rather than silver.

Mounted on a typically small Indian horse, **B3** has a conventional light dragoon-style jacket of the period with blue facings, and white lace arranged in chevrons; once again the turnbacks are facing-coloured rather than white. Again, all the accoutrements are European, including the rather short-bladed sabre carried instead of the more traditional *tulwar*. Another Green watercolour in the series depicts an officer, presumably belonging to the same regiment, wearing a very similar uniform but with gold lace substituted for white on both the coat and shabraque, although the diagonal band on

Sepoy of 3rd Bombay Native Infantry, depicted in a well-known engraving by M. Darley, 1773. The jacket is presumably red and made with 'European cloth' faced with blue; at this early date the rest of his clothing is local.

the turban remains white. He also carries what appears to be an Indian-style standard, the details of which are unclear, with a silver crescent finial.

C: 1790–1800

C1: Bengal *sepoy*, 1790s
C2: Private, 2nd Madras Europeans, 1780s
C3: Eurasian fifer, c.1800

The Bengal sepoy **C1** is based on a series of sketches by an unknown artist (perhaps Green), this time dating from the 1790s. The uniform is still similar to that worn by the Carnatic troops in the 1780s although there are noticeable differences in the shape and size of the turban, and the *jangheas* are much shorter. Note the leaf-shaped 'badge' rising from the turban with a unit or company designation in a local script; this feature is often rendered in contemporary prints as an acutely pointed triangle – hence the nickname 'sundial' turbans. Again the battalion is unidentified, but it must belong to the 1st Brigade formed in 1775, as all seven consecutively-numbered battalions in the brigade had blue facings. The 2nd Bde, comprising the 8th–14th BNI, had black facings, and the 3rd Bde green.

The 2nd Madras Europeans were distinguished from Lawrence's original battalion by wearing of black facings, probably inherited from Eyre Coote's 84th Foot which provided most of its original personnel. **C2** is largely based on a sketch by a Company artist actually depicting a Madras artilleryman some time in the late 1780s, but the basic outline of the uniform appears to have been the same for both infantry and gunners. In December 1776 the 'necessaries' issued to each soldier on the Madras establishment still included two pairs of conventionally cut breeches 'made full, to come up well upon the belly, and to cover the knees'; but soldiers were also given two pairs of 'pantaloons, two pair of stockings', and a 'pair of black gaiters to button' – although those depicted in the sketch are white. The then commander-in-chief, MajGen Stuart, genially conceded 'that in respect to the dress of the soldier he does not expect all the precision and exactness of a European parade, he knows the climate will not admit of it, but he expects a uniform soldier-like appearance in the whole army, answerable to the means afforded by the Honourable Company'. Lord Cornwallis, on the other hand, professed himself horrified.

A trio of figures in a well-known watercolour sketch dated to c.1800 is the basis for **C3**. The two fifers and the drummer in the original sketch wear an interesting mix of European and Indian garments, reflected in the Eurasian features of at least one of them. The turban is of the 'sundial' style common up to the early years of the 19th century, but the musicians' coat with its false hanging sleeves would have been regarded as outmoded in the regular army even in the 1790s. Unusually for a unit with blue facings, the colours are completely reversed. Drummers and fifers of British units with blue facings always wore red coats distinguished only by the addition of large quantities of drummers' lace, but here a facing-coloured blue coat is worn. The large (but quite typical) brass fife case is worthy of note; the drummer in the original sketch also had a plain brass-shelled drum rather than the painted wood normally favoured by British units – probably because brass was rather less susceptible to being eaten by insects.

D: BRITISH OFFICERS, 1790s–1800
D1: Lieutenant-colonel, 7th Madras Native Cavalry, 1790s
D2: Officer in hussar jacket, 1799
D3: Officer in service dress, c.1800

For some reason red jackets, as well as red turbans, continued to be favoured by the Madras Native Cavalry long after their Bengal colleagues had adopted blue (or rather 'cavalry-grey') dolmans. The scarlet uniform is illustrated to perfection in **D1**, based on Sir Henry Raeburn's portrait of LtCol William Shirreff of the 7th MNC. Broadly speaking the style is identical to that being worn by regular Light Dragoons, Fencibles and other volunteer light cavalry at home, although the dolman is obviously worn open as a concession to the climate, and the leopard-skin 'turban' on his Tarleton helmet (obscured at this angle) also hints at some more exotic posting than his native Stirlingshire. While undoubtedly worn, the relatively heavy Tarleton was understandably unpopular in India, and most European cavalry officers preferred a lighter, classically styled helmet with a red horsehair mane.

The quite unique style of hussar jacket worn by **D2** appears in a number of paintings and other illustrations of East India Company officers dating from the 1790s and early 1800s. It was single-breasted, decorated with a cord braiding more usually associated with hussars or light dragoons, and was invariably worn open or at least fastened with just one or two buttons on the breast. It bears some resemblance to a hussar-style over-jacket called a 'kit' worn by some British light dragoons in the early 1790s, and so may conceivably have been based either upon that or on an imagined Hungarian original. At any rate it was clearly intended as a comfortable but stylish garment, unmistakeably European in origin but yet far better adapted to local conditions than the traditional double-breasted regimental coat. It seems to have been adopted not only by EIC officers but also by a number of King's officers who had spent some time in India. A notable example

was Sir David Baird, who was twice depicted wearing such a jacket, both in a contemporary engraving depicting the surrender of the Mysore princes at Seringapatam in 1799 and in a rather later posthumous portrait by David Wilkie.

The very much more workmanlike **D3** is primarily based on two figures standing in the foreground of a painting of Trichinopoly by Philip Le Couten. One is depicted as here, and the other with a fur-roached hat like that worn by D2, although similar figures also appear in contemporary sketches of East India troops serving under Baird in Egypt. The red-over-black hackle in this officer's hat is noteworthy but unexplained. The short-tailed, single-breasted jacket is a style authorized for all infantry officers of the British Army in October 1797. For some reason it immediately proved unpopular at home and was ordered to be discontinued there as from 24 December 1798; however, a number of sketches and other illustrations show it still being worn as a service dress by officers serving in the West Indies, and in July 1806 a tail-less version – or shell jacket – was officially authorized for wear by Bombay officers.

E: INFANTRY, 1805–14
E1: Havildar, Bengal Native Infantry, 1814
E2: Private, Bengal Europeans, 1811
E3: Sepoy, 1st Bombay Native Infantry, 1805

Based on a print by Charles Hamilton Smith, **E1** now displays his rank conventionally by the three tapes on his sleeve and the worsted waist-sash with a central facing-

coloured stripe, just like his European counterparts. Once again he carries a firelock and normal infantry accoutrements rather than a pole-arm, as presumably was the case with his counterparts in the Company's European infantry units. A more subtle distinction of rank, however, may also be the wearing of long *jodhpurs* or pantaloons. These were originally worn only by *subedars* (captains) and *jemadars* (lieutenants), but the privilege was extended to *havildars* in the Bengal Army in 1801. Hamilton Smith emphasizes this distinction in his plate by depicting a *sepoy* in *jangheas*; however, in some Bengal units all ranks had already been wearing them for some time in cold weather, and in June 1813 permission was granted for them to be worn all year round in preference to the old-fashioned shorts.

Amidst the increasing Westernization of the uniforms which followed the formation of regular units, the traditional turban remained the most important distinguishing feature of Indian troops. The original 'sundial' style was a genuine turban solidly formed of tightly wound strips of cloth, but the new version introduced in Madras in 1806 was a bell-shaped construction of blue cloth stretched over a rattan or bamboo armature. By cocking it over and retaining the decorative white bands of

Sepoy of Madras Native Infantry, c.1850. Only the shako-like false turban and the sandals distinguish him from his British counterparts – see Plate G1.

the old one it still retained some semblance of the original, but to all intents and purposes it was a shako – and in Indian eyes a European hat, and uncomfortable to boot! Consequently its introduction provoked a short but bloody mutiny at Vellore, leading to some minor improvements in the initial design. Bengal units also adopted a very similar one in about 1810, but those worn in Bombay were at first very distinctive.

For some reason Hamilton Smith neglected to provide a plate depicting any of the Company's European regiments, and **E2** is therefore based on one of the illustrations in Abraham James' *Analytical View of the Manual and Platoon Exercises*, published in Calcutta in 1811. While Capt James belonged to the regular 67th Foot his book was illustrated with sketches of Company troops, of both European and Native units, at which it was aimed. His illustrations show the coatees to be rather old-fashioned in appearance, being cut away from the lowest button rather than running straight across at the front. It is also interesting to note that while Hamilton's Smith's uniform charts accompanying his series of plates imply that the Company's Europeans had the same lace loops on the chest of their coatees as those worn by their Native colleagues, Capt James depicts the trio on which this plate is based as wearing plain-fronted coatees with lace on the collar, shoulder straps and cuffs only. James' illustrations also depict the same shako as worn by regulars now adopted by Company troops in place of the old linen hats 'suitable to the climate'. Presumably these were in turn replaced by the false-fronted 1812 or 'Belgic' shako, which were originally prescribed in white for troops serving in the tropics. A Company artillery officer's cap-plate for that pattern survives, but otherwise there appears to be no visual evidence for its general use before the introduction of the more popular bell-topped styles.

E3 is based on a watercolour of c.1805, with the turban worn by infantry on the Bombay establishment. The body of the turban resembled that worn by some Native Cavalry units and the brass plate on the front, similar to that worn by North German fusilier units, was originally a grenadier company distinction. In 1796, however, it was ordered to be worn by all companies and was to bear the regimental number on the front – or an anchor in the case of the Marine Battalion. Troops from the other Presidencies tended to be rather unkind about this odd turban, and it was replaced by a more conventional one in about 1814, though still with decorative chinscales and the number on the front. Note that the very long *jangheas* worn in Bombay are to all intents and purposes kneebreeches.

F: NATIVE CAVALRY
F1: Farrier, Skinner's Horse
F2: *Sowar*, Bengal Native Cavalry, 1814
F3: *Sowar*, Java Light Cavalry or 4th MNC, 1812–15
The most famous of the many units of irregular cavalry raised by the Bengal Army was undoubtedly Capt James Skinner's corps. Skinner, a Eurasian, was so successful that by 1823 he was given a British regular commission as lieutenant-colonel and his corps was split into two separate units, the 1st and 3rd Bengal Local Horse. Skinner and his officers normally wore old-fashioned British light cavalry uniforms with dark blue braided dolmans and Tarleton helmets, but the rank-and-file wore very distinctive plain yellow coats called *alkalaks*, which earned them the nickname of the 'Yellow Boys' – significantly, the wearing of yellow garments by Rajputs was a sign that they intended to fight to the death. This garment is usefully illustrated by the farrier **F1**, depicted by a contemporary Company artist. His headgear – apparently an ordinary military cap covered with fur – is obviously peculiar to his appointment. Troopers generally favoured traditionally-wound *pugris* of red cloth or Persian-style helmets, and sometimes also wore short-sleeved red jackets trimmed with black fur over their *alkalaks*, presumably to help identify whose side they were on. Weapons were equally traditional, comprising lances, *tulwars*, shields and even matchlocks.

There were eight regiments of regular Bengal Native Cavalry by 1806, and the *sowar* **F2**, based on another plate by Charles Hamilton Smith, wears the uniform common to them all. The braided dolman was in a blueish-grey colour variously described as 'French grey' or 'cavalry grey'. Unlike the Madras Native Cavalry, who were variously distinguished by pale yellow, orange, buff and deep yellow facings, all but one of the Bengal regiments had orange facings, at this period displayed on collar and cuffs. The rather bulbous dark blue turban was – like those worn by sepoys in the infantry and *golundaz* in the artillery – not a true wound *pugri* but a fairly light headdress worn in imitation of one. The high jacked leather boots seem a little incongruous for light cavalry, but were affected by many Indian cavalry and horse artillery units both at the time and long afterwards. Otherwise the weapons and equipment, including the 1796 pattern light cavalry sword, are entirely typical of regular British light dragoons. The Governor General's Bodyguard, also depicted by Hamilton Smith, wore a very similar uniform but with a red jacket faced with dark blue. European officers, as depicted in D1, wore the same uniform but continued to substitute either a Tarleton helmet, or more commonly a lighter locally-made one, for the turban.

The Java Light Cavalry, **F3**, and its accompanying troop of horse artillery were formed in 1812 specifically to serve as part of the garrison of that newly conquered island. Sometimes confused with an entirely different unit of Java Hussars recruited from Europeans on the island, this was part of the Bengal Army. Commanded by Maj Lucius O'Brien of the 8th BNC, it comprised three troops of volunteers drawn from all eight Bengal regiments. The unit served on the island until 1815 when the Governor, Sir Stamford Raffles, decided it was an unnecessary extravagance and had it returned to India, where it was eventually broken up and the personnel were returned to their original regiments. The uniform worn is surprisingly problematic, and – as tentatively reconstructed here, after Hamilton Smith – it may have been quite distinctive. In outline it obviously conformed to the general style of Native cavalry regiments, but the turban is shown by Hamilton Smith as red rather than dark blue, while the dolman is dark blue rather than cavalry-grey. Furthermore, although Hamilton Smith depicted the facings as deep yellow, the *Calcutta Annual Register and Directory* for 1814 listed them as white. It is therefore likely that the identification of the uniform in his plate is erroneous, and that the combination of dark blue dolman with deep yellow facings and a red turban indicates not a Java volunteer at all, but a sowar of the 4th Madras Native Cavalry.

G: THE SEPOY ARMY, 1820–35
G1: *Sepoy*, 40th Madras Native Infantry, 1835
G2: *Sepoy*, 1st Madras Pioneers, 1835
G3: Trooper, 1st Rohilla Cavalry, 1820s

From the 1820s onwards the Westernization of sepoy uniforms continued to gather pace, as seen in these figures largely based on paintings by a Company artist of soldiers in the Madras Army in 1835. **G1** manages to look remarkably like a contemporary soldier of the regular 68th (Durham) Light Infantry, and in reality is distinguished from one only by the badge on his breastplate, the wearing of sandals rather than boots, and by his turban, which had more or less reached its final, almost cylindrical shape and is to all intents and purposes a peakless shako. (Although it was originally remodelled in this form to resemble the headdress of European infantry, both British regulars and the Company's European regiments were now wearing bell-topped rather than cylindrical caps.) In practice the distinction was becoming increasingly immaterial; so unpopular were these turbans that they were generally reserved for formal parades and guard-mountings, and most other duties were carried out wearing an unambiguously European Kilmarnock-style forage cap, with a white cover for hot weather. That cap in fact replaced turbans entirely in the Bengal Army in 1847, although the Bombay Army retained its turbans until 1854, and the Madras Army had them up to the end.

Like other armies the Company raised units of military labourers. These were variously titled Lascars, Pioneers, or Sappers and Miners, and were commanded by officers seconded from the Engineers. For the most part they followed British Army uniform practice, with blue jackets faced with black in the early days giving way to red faced with blue. However, the 1st Madras Pioneers had the unique uniform depicted in **G2**, with a jacket of Rifle-green faced with black. Also of interest is the way in which the traditional tools of the job, including in this case an axe and fascine-knife, are carried on the waist belt; the shoulder belt presumably carries a bayonet.

The 1st Rohilla Cavalry, re-titled the 3rd Bengal Local Horse in 1824, were a typical irregular cavalry regiment; as depicted in **G3**, the *sowars* and Indian officers wore *alkalaks* and festooned themselves with whatever weapons took their fancy. The curious *tarboosh* headdress was originally worn by the first units of regular Madras Native Cavalry before the adoption of the bulbous 'turban' seen in Plate F, and those worn by the Rohillas may even have been rescued from a forgotten store for use on formal occasions – ordinarily they wore dark blue *pugris*. British officers at first wore a European-style uniform, and a portrait of Maj George Cunningham shows a scarlet jacket with black facings and gold braid, with a red-maned helmet. Later it became increasingly common for officers assigned to these irregular units to wear the same costume as their men, including *pugris*.

H: EUROPEANS, 1840S
H1: Officer, 1st Bombay Lancers, 1842
H2: Private, 1st Madras Fusiliers, 1843
H3: Officer, Madras Horse Artillery, 1846

Two contemporaneous officer portraits provide the basis for **H1**. Originally raised as a single troop in 1803, the unit was expanded into a full regiment in 1817, which until 1842 appeared in the *East India Register* as the 1st Bombay Light

'Sergeant of Light Infantry and Private of Madrass Sepoys', by Charles Hamilton Smith, 1815 – compare with Plate E1. Both men wear the characteristic 1806 pattern blue turban, and shorts decorated just above the ends of the legs with two narrow blue lines. The jackets closely follow British patterns, except that the sergeant's flank company wings are in his regiment's green facing colour.

Cavalry. Even after its conversion to a lancer regiment – which may actually have taken place slightly earlier – the cap plate and sabretache still bore the letters 'B.L.C.'. The uniform is identical in style to that adopted by some British light dragoon regiments on their conversion to lancers shortly after the Napoleonic Wars, but is immediately distinguished by the colour and by the red-topped lance cap. According to the Bombay Dress Regulations of 1850 the regiment should have been wearing the cavalry-grey prescribed for most of the Company's cavalry units since the turn of the century, with white facings. This may well have been the case for the rank-and-file, but both officers are depicted in a surprisingly bright shade of blue. Otherwise, in all three presidencies most European cavalry officers continued to wear hussar-style dolmans, but the crested and maned helmets gave way to light dragoon-style shakoes. In Bombay this occurred as early as 1824, with Bengal following suit in 1830, but Madras officers – officially at least – clung to their helmets until 1846. *Sowars* also continued to wear conventional uniforms including turbans, although, as in Bengal, these were discontinued in favour of Kilmarnock-style caps, usually worn with

Bandmaster and musicians of the Madras Army, 1841. As in the British Army, all bandsmen at this date wore white coatees irrespective of their regiment. In EIC units most bandsmen were traditionally recruited from Eurasians, who at this period were considered socially superior to Indians but no longer acceptable as fighting soldiers in European units – an example of the increasing racial prejudice of the Victorian age.

white cotton covers; a contemporary illustration of the 3rd BLC at Koosh-ab in 1856 also appears to show neck-covers worn by all ranks. The sabretache, according to the same regulations, was to be of white Morocco leather with the face covered with cavalry-grey cloth (i.e. the same colour as the uniform), trimmed around with 2¼in silver lace and bearing the letters 'B.L.C.' embroidered in the centre and surmounted by a star. Although not mentioned in the regulations, a pair of crossed lances surrounded by a wreath also appeared behind the 'official' device.

The cheerful roughneck depicted as **H2** provides a stark contrast to all this finery. In 1843 the 1st Madras European Regiment was designated as the Madras Fusiliers and given dark blue facings marking its quasi-royal status – also underlined by the addition of a crown above the elephant on the breastplates. While broadly conforming to contemporary regular uniforms there remained some subtle differences. The most notable were the rather plain facing-coloured wings and shoulder straps, in this case sporting a flaming grenade badge indicating their status as Fusiliers; the pointed rather

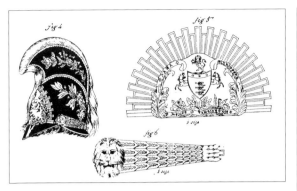

Madras Horse Artillery officer's helmet as depicted in the 1842 Dress Regulations – see Plate H3. This is very similar to the final pattern of helmet worn by light cavalry officers just prior to the adoption of a shako in the 1830s.

than round cuffs; and an absence of lace on their jackets – or at least, on those worn on service. The EIC's European troops were still notoriously tough, and (with due allowance for the exertions of marching in this climate) this figure based on a sketch by a Captain Ryves seems to show a rather rough-and-ready attitude to soldiering; note the turned-down collar, discarded neck-stock and native sandals.

Since no European cavalry units survived after the very early days, it was the Company's Horse Artillery who set out to lend the necessary fashionable tone to the proceedings, and **H3** provides a splendid example. In this case the uniform displays significant differences between regular army and Company army practice. The braided dolman was common to both services, but while the Royal Horse Artillery officers affected a hussar-style uniform, Company ones preferred this elegant 'Roman' helmet with its vivid scarlet horse-hair mane ('to be cut horizontally in line with the bottom of the ear'). The Bombay Horse Artillery wore a very similar uniform and helmet, but were distinguished by a black mane and a cheetah-skin 'turban' on the helmet. The Bengal Horse Artillery wore a red mane but were distinguished from their Madras colleagues by a leopard-skin turban with gilt chains, and a 'brush' on the peak of the crest. In about 1855 this was to have been superseded by a seal-skin busby cap of the style worn by the Royal Horse Artillery, but although a solitary example exists this never seems to have caught on. The thigh-length jacked leather boots affected by most Company cavalry units were worn in full dress and occasionally on service as well, with white breeches, but ordinarily trousers were preferred. These were supposed to be sky-blue or white according to season until July 1846, when the dark blue ones shown here were substituted for winter sky-blue. The undress uniform was scarcely less magnificent, with either a dark blue shell jacket laced in gold, or a blue frock-coat with black silk braid loops and olivettes, worn over a scarlet waistcoat, and with a forage cap as illustrated. Indian personnel likewise wore light cavalry-style uniforms in dark blue rather than cavalry-grey; interestingly, in addition to their usual distinctions of rank Indian officers had red turbans in contrast to the blue worn by the rank-and-file. As in the other presidencies there was also a tendency to replace the turban with a Kilmarnock cap when off the parade ground.

INDEX

Figures in **bold** refer to illustrations.